THE LIONESS WITHIN

Outcome Journal

DEBORAH BLAKEY

The Lioness Within Outcome Journal
By Deborah Blakey

ISBN #: 979-8-9868110-1-7

Author: Deborah Blakey
Cover Design & Layout Design: Velin@Perseus-Design.com
Publisher: Power2Excel Agency, LLC

Printed in the United States of America.

CATEGORY: Self-Help/Personal Growth/Success

DEDICATION

To my nieces and nephews. You are the legacy builders for the next generation.

Always know there is life after any hardship, failure, and setback, no matter where you come from or where you started. You control how your story ends. Look at your aunts or your uncles and learn from us. It's time for you all to stand up for and with each other. Realize you are a part of this big family. We are all we got. Repeat it when you see each other. Repeat it when you remember that we made it. We are all we got. That is our mantra.

To all who read this Outcome Journal, when I look back at my 21-year-old self, I would tell her to stop running from God, Run to him. He has what you are craving. He has what you need. He is the love you were missing when your mother went home to Him at a young age. He is your Heavenly Father who took the place of the earthly father who was not there. He was your forever husband when the divorces seemed too much. Only He can love you the way you want and need and deserve. God has been waiting with open arms that entire time I was looking in all the wrong places. So trust the process and trust God.

I love you, and I mean it, and there's absolutely nothing you can do about it.

To the Lioness Within You!

TABLE OF CONTENTS

PROLOGUE

When I think about a Lioness, I think about how strong we are as women, so I encourage you to embrace your inner Lioness and roar with strength and grace. There is great power in just being you. You are enough. Just as a lioness protects her pride and stands fiercely in the face of adversity, you too can stand tall and strong in your convictions defending your beliefs and championing your dreams.

What will be your call to action today that will catapult you into your tomorrow?

Life is like a book. It is filled with many chapters: happy, sad, exciting embarrassing; as well as fearful and challenging wins and losses. Each chapter represents a different phase of our lives, and we cannot always control what happens in each one. But we can choose how to respond. And just like a book, the story of our lives is never finished. We have the power to turn the page and start a new chapter to start over on our narrative.

What will you do today to shape your destiny?

Come along with me and embrace the chapters of your lives with courage, curiosity, and an open heart for God to mend the broken places and bring forth that Lioness within.

Your story is your background; the trials, upbringing, and everything you've done up until now that led you to this point. You have a powerful story. You have a voice. Your story made you who you are for better or for worse right now, including the struggles and obstacles that got in the way that you pushed to the side and made your way through. Your life experiences or someone else's lessons and personal stories will resonate and free someone else.

It's time to leave your comfort zone and take that leap of faith. Will you do this with me?

HOW TO USE THIS OUTCOME JOURNAL

This Outcome Journal is designed for women who have experienced brokenness and are ready to unleash their inner lioness. It provides practical tools and exercises to help women build their confidence and achieve their goals, with Christ as their foundation. Through self-reflection, prayer, devotion, and empowerment, this journal will help women transform their brokenness into strength and resilience, freeing them to live their best lives.

To get the most out of the Outcome Journal, allow 20 to 30 minutes daily to study. Set a definite time and select a quiet place to explore without interruption. Keep a Bible at hand to find scriptures as directed in the journal.

Using the Word of God to remember who you are and who God says you are, is key to making the most of this journal. For the activity and assignment section, write down your thoughts on how the study shifted your belief or ideas about who you are and how God has always shown up for you.

WHO IS THE LIONESS WITHIN?

The Lioness is a mother, a female, and a queen. The Lioness is a magnificent image of strength, passion, and beauty. She stands as a fierce defender of her family and a more than capable provider. In groups, the lioness becomes a creative and strategic force to be reckoned with, acting as one to change the world around them.

You are a Lioness Reflection
You have made it through many storms in life, and you're still standing!

Reflect and write down some dark lonely places you have overcome and stop and feel the strength and power it took to stand.

Evaluate and Elevate
Is there something about how you think contributng to the distractions in your life?

Are you continually going in circles? If yes, it's time to evaluate your thinking.

Where your mind goes, your life will follow.

Did you know there's a you inside of you - a you, you haven't met yet?

Are you so busy that you haven't taken the time to get to know yourself? Do you have a vision problem or maybe a value problem?

It is impossible to outperform the picture that you hold in your mind of yourself!

In Numbers 13:31-33, the Israelites have been called to step out in faith and into the promised land, trusting in God's promise. However, when surveying the land and the enemies that lived there, the Israelites said, "We seem like grasshoppers in our own eyes." Now that assessment may seem incomprehensible to us, reading and knowing the miracles God performed for the Israelites: i.e., the parting of the Red Sea, providing water for them in the desert and witnessing the glory of the Lord descending upon Mount Sinai.

WHAT IS YOUR I AM?

The Hebrews definition of “I AM” means, “it came to pass.” We must guard our mouths when making this command, for “I AM” is a confirmation. When you say, “I AM,” you are commanding what follows to come to pass. You are releasing the power of Jesus to come to pass. Our words are on assignment. We have been made in God’s image. What we release goes out into the atmosphere. They will not return void.

Activity

Affirmations are powerful. Reflect on what is your I AM. Then, write your I AM Affirmations below.

THE LIONESS WITHIN PROMISE

To unleash the Lioness Within, we ask you to dedicate yourself to God to make the most of the study. By signing this promise, you pledge to adopt these practices as you study.

As a Lioness, I promise to:

1. Trust God's way more than my thoughts. (Proverbs 3:5-6)

2. Walk into my purpose according to God's will. (1 Peter 2:9)

3. Trust God's promise for my life. (Jeremiah 29:11)

4. Cultivate a deeper relationship with God. (John 15:4-)

5. Always go to God first in all situations and circumstances. (James 1:5)

6. Set my mind on greater things ahead. (Luke 1:45; Proverbs 31:25)

7. Trust God to align me with the right people in my life. (1 Corinthians 11:11-12)

8. Pray daily. (1 Thessalonians 5:16-18)

9. Speak kindly about myself and others around me. (Proverbs 31:26)

10. Have daily quiet time to hear God's voice. (James 4:8)

11. Share my faith and testimony with others. (Psalm 96:2-4)

12. Have confidence in myself so that others may see God's glory through me. (Deuteronomy 31:6)

You can include other promises you hope to keep to yourself as you unleash the lioness within you.

____

____

____

____

Person's Name Sign: __________________________

Date: __________________________________

THE LIONESS WITHIN WORKSHEET

This worksheet allows you to reflect on your journey and who you are. You must challenge yourself, to be honest about the parts of your journey that shaped you into the woman you are today. Jot down any brief thoughts that come to mind.

What is Your Story?

1. How have you become the woman you are today? What person(s) and event(s) influenced you the most?

____

____

____

____

2. What event stands out in your mind about your journey? Write all the parts of your story that make you smile, laugh, break your heart, and have moments where you have felt hope.

____

____

____

____

3. What is one thing about your journey to share as a testimony?

DEBORAH BLAKEY

OUTCOME JOURNAL

Introduction

INTRODUCTION

This study will help you understand what it means to make God your foundation and allow you to commit to trusting God in all circumstances and situations.

1. What are you trusting Him to do? How do you want Him to show up for you?

2. God can take all the broken pieces of your heart and thoughts and make something beautiful. What event(s) has left you feeling like you are not good enough? How do you hope God will mend the broken pieces of your heart and restore your faith so that your life will be transformed?

3. How has God shown up for you when you least expected it? Reflect on the moments leading up to that moment and how he turned a less desirable situation into a life-changing moment. Did he align the people to be there for you when you felt lost, alone, or as if your life was falling apart?

ACTIVITY

Write a letter to God, believing He will heal your broken pieces. Spend time reflecting on your journey and how you want God to lead you to a place of growth, confidence, and assurance that He will never leave or forsake you.

Write down everything you want God to do in your life.

DEBORAH BLAKEY

OUTCOME JOURNAL

Chapter One

CHAPTER ONE:

IT WASN'T SUPPOSED TO TURN OUT THIS WAY (BROKEN AND SCARED)

God is the only one who can put us back together and make us whole. Jeremiah 17:14 says, "Heal me, O Lord, and I shall be healed; Save me, and I shall be saved, For You are my praise."

Sometimes it can feel like your entire life has shattered, especially if you have gone through a testing moment or traumatic experience. These times can make you feel ashamed and want to hide instead of showing up as the person He intended you to be.

Despite our perceptions of our lives and experiences, everything is orchestrated perfectly according to God's will. Therefore, even our brokenness can be restored into something more beautiful than we imagine. This brokenness can come from various circumstances, whether the result of our choices or events beyond our control.

Your Latter Shall be Greater than Your Former

Cultivate some time to reflect on your childhood; what thoughts arise when you begin to reflect? Who is the person(s) who influenced your life the most? How do you believe your childhood led you to where you are today?

REFLECT ON THIS: EMBRACE EVERY PART OF YOUR STORY

What is God showing you about the story you need to embrace? How does it make you feel? Are you ashamed, broken, or healed?

Pray about the parts of your story you have been hiding and want to be healed.

1. What past struggles or traumatic experiences have shifted and affected you? How has it chipped away who you are or want to be?

2. Is this experience still showing up in your life? If yes, how so?

3. “I also know it was God who strengthened me for this role.” How do you believe God is crafting your life to accomplish a big mission?

4. To embrace my story, I need to ____________________

REFLECT ON THIS: EMBRACE EVERY PART OF YOUR STORY

- **Spend time with God**

Cultivate extra quiet time to sit with your thoughts and read the Word.

- **Pray in Faith**

Use the scripture to pray about God's plans for your life. Where are you feeling led to next? Is it to share parts of your story with others? Write the thoughts and revelations that come to you.

Scripture: Jeremiah 29:11, "For I know the plans I have for you," declares the LORD, "plans to prosper you and not to harm you, plans to give you hope and a future."

FIVE AFFIRMATIONS

1. I am who God says I am.
2. I am a Child of God, and greatness lies within me.
3. I am created with a purpose that God will guide me to accomplish in this lifetime.
4. I am made in the image of God
5. I am a vessel for which God is doing wondrous works.

DEBORAH BLAKEY

OUTCOME JOURNAL

Chapter Two

CHAPTER TWO:

MY FIRST LOVE

As Christians, our relationship with God is the foundation of our faith and the compass that guides us through life's ups and downs. We know we need to prioritize our relationship with God above all else, but sometimes, we can become distracted by other relationships. Whether it's our dating life, the health of our marriage, or our family relationships, these connections can take on an importance that overshadows our connection to God.

It's important to remember that these relationships are not mutually exclusive from our relationship with God. Our relationships with others can reflect our walk with the Lord. When prioritizing our relationship with God, we learn to love others selflessly, forgive freely, and extend grace and compassion. Our relationships with others can also bring us closer to God as we share our struggles and joys and support each other through life's challenges.

However, we must not allow these relationships to become idols. We should continually evaluate our priorities and ensure we put God first in all our lives, including our relationships. As we seek to grow in our relationship with God, He will guide us in our interactions with others, and we will see the fruit of our faithfulness in our relationships.

REFLECT ON THIS: WHAT TAKES PRIORITY?

Relationships

Which relationship takes priority in your life?
Has this relationship always been a priority?

If not, why is it a priority, and if you should change it, who would you cultivate a better relationship with and why?

1. What are some ways you willingly took on a role in your life but later realized that you were not mentally mature enough to handle it? How did this impact your relationships and growth? Reflect on how you moved forward from this experience and what steps you took to ensure you were better prepared for future challenges.

2. Who was the first example of love in your life? How did their actions and words shape your understanding and love experience ever since? Reflect on this person's impact on your life and how their example of love has influenced how you love and interact with others today. Consider how you can use the lessons you learned from this person to cultivate more profound and meaningful relationships in your life.

Disruptions and God's Alignment

1. "Do not remember the former things, Nor consider the things of old. Behold, I will do a new thing, Now it shall spring forth; Shall you not know it? I will even make a road in the wilderness And rivers in the desert" (Isaiah 43:18-19). Describe an event(s) that you believe disrupted your life. How do you believe God realigned your plans for his plans and his purpose for your life?

2. Which scripture gives you hope that God will never leave or forsake you despite disruptions in your life?

ACTIVITY

Share your story/testimony about how God used disruption to realign his plans for a greater purpose.

FIVE AFFIRMATIONS ON RELATIONSHIPS FOR THE LIONESS WITHIN

1. God's love for me is unconditional and never-ending, and I am worthy of His love and affection.

2. As I seek God's guidance, He will lead me to the right relationships to honor and glorify Him.

3. Through my relationships, God teaches me valuable lessons about love and grace.

4. I am called to love others as God loves me and extends grace and forgiveness even when difficult.

5. God's love is the foundation for all healthy and fulfilling relationships.

FIVE AFFIRMATIONS ON DISRUPTION AND GOD'S ALIGNMENT FOR THE LIONESS WITHIN

1. I trust in God's plan for my life, even when it involves disruption or change that I don't fully understand.

2. In times of disruption, I seek God's guidance and trust that He will lead me on the best path for me.

3. God's alignment is always for my highest good, and I trust He is working all things together for my benefit.

4. Even when I face unexpected challenges, I can find peace and comfort in God's persistent presence and love.

Disruption allows me to grow and deepen my relationship with God as I rely on His strength and guidance to navigate difficult times.

DEBORAH BLAKEY

OUTCOME JOURNAL

Chapter Three

CHAPTER THREE:

MY SOUL CRIES OUT

When we experience brokenness, it can feel like our world has come crashing down. The pain and confusion can be overwhelming, leaving us feeling lost and alone. At times like this, it's common for our souls to cry out for healing and relief.

When your heart is broken, it may feel like an exhausting burden. However, if you surrender your worries and concerns to God, He will provide you with the support and strength needed to overcome any pain and suffering. God is the ultimate source of healing, and by placing your trust in Him, you can find solace and restoration. So lean on Him, and rest assured that He will grant you the closure and peace you seek.

Matthew 11:28 “Come to me, all you who are weary and burdened, and I will give you rest.”

Some of my most painful experiences came from those I believe should have loved me wholly. Instead, it wasn't always the case.

REFLECT ON THIS: GOD'S LIGHT IS ON YOU

Brokenness

1. "Uncle Slim would always reach out to me, and we became close. I don't know why my father never did; it just never sat right with me that he never wanted to get to know me or his other kids." How can you lean on God during times of brokenness and find solace and restoration? Think about a moment in your life that made you feel heartbroken by someone who should have loved and cared for you fully.

2. What does Matthew 11:28 teach you about finding rest in God, even in the midst of burdens?

3. What are some ways you have tried to find rest and relief outside of God when feeling heartbroken and weary?

4. How can you strengthen your faith in God and learn to trust Him more fully during challenging times?

REFLECT ON THIS: GOD RESTORES THE BROKEN

Who was the first person to break your heart? How do you hope God will restore your broken heart? Share your deepest thoughts with the Lord and ask for his hands of restoration, "The LORD is close to the brokenhearted; he rescues those whose spirits are crushed. " - Psalm 34:14

ACTIVITY

Share your story/testimony about how God used your broken heart to realign his plans for a greater purpose.

DEBORAH BLAKEY

OUTCOME JOURNAL

Chapter Four

CHAPTER FOUR:

LIVING TO DIE

Life is full of ups and downs, and sometimes we find ourselves in moments of darkness, feeling lost, overwhelmed, and hopeless.

During these difficult times, seeing the light at the end of the tunnel can be challenging, and we may struggle to find a way out of the darkness. However, as Christians, we can take comfort in knowing that God is always with us, even in our darkest moments. He is the one who can shine light into our darkness and guide us toward the path of healing and restoration.

With His love and grace, we can find hope, strength, and peace amidst the turmoil and emerge from the darkness stronger and more resilient than ever.

REFLECT ON THIS: GOD'S LIGHT IS ON YOU

God will always show us that you can't put your happiness, joy, deliverance, healing, and peace in no one other than Him. What practical steps can we take to remind ourselves of God's promises and focus on Him during difficult seasons?

Leaning on Your Community

1. "You know God is with you when he sends you not one, but four powerful sister friends. Real friends, ride-or-die friends." How can you effectively communicate your struggles and ask for support from your community?

2. How can you offer support and encouragement to others who may be going through difficult times?

Shining Light Even in Your Darkest Moments

1. What are some giants you are facing now? How do you trust God to be a light in your dark moments?

2. What biblical verses provide comfort and hope during challenging times?

3. How can we cultivate a deeper relationship with God to receive His light in our dark moments?

ACTIVITY

Identify your community of believers who can pour into you when you feel like you're in your dark moments or the lowest season. Cultivate a habit of asking for help versus isolating yourself when moments can be challenging.

Pray and ask God to align you with the right people for every season.

FIVE AFFIRMATIONS

1. God's favor is upon me, and I am blessed beyond measure.

2. I trust in God's plan for my life, knowing that His favor goes before me in all that I do.

3. With God's favor, I am empowered to overcome any obstacle and achieve my goals.

4. I am worthy of God's favor, not because of my merit, but because of His love and grace towards me.

5. As a daughter of the Most High, I walk in the confidence and authority that comes with knowing I have God's favor.

DEBORAH BLAKEY

OUTCOME JOURNAL

Chapter Five

CHAPTER FIVE:

BEAUTY FOR ASHES

Sometimes in life, we can feel stuck or lost, wondering if anything will ever change or if we'll always feel stuck in the same place. But the good news is that God is always at work, even amid our most difficult and challenging circumstances. And often, when we least expect it, He does something new in our lives that brings hope, healing, and transformation.

Isaiah 43:19 says, "Behold, I am doing a new thing; now it springs forth, do you not perceive it? I will make a way in the wilderness and rivers in the desert." This verse reminds us that God is always at work, even in our most barren and desolate places. He can bring about new life and growth where we thought there was only emptiness and despair.

For women stuck or struggling to find a way forward, this promise from Isaiah can be a source of great hope and encouragement. No matter how impossible our circumstances may seem, God is able to make a way where there seems to be no way. He can bring beauty from ashes and new life from the most unlikely places.

So if you feel like you're in a wilderness or a desert place, take heart. God is doing a new thing and making way for you. Keep your eyes open for the further growth and opportunities that are coming forth, and trust that God is leading you toward a brighter future.

REFLECT ON THIS: GOD WILL DO A NEW THING

Reflect on times in your life when God has done a new thing or brought about unexpected blessings. What did you learn from those experiences?

A NEW DAY HAS COME: LIONESS COME FORTH

1. How can you cultivate an attitude of expectancy and hope amid uncertainty or difficult circumstances?

2. What steps can you take to align your will and desires with God's plan for your life?

3. How can you trust God's faithfulness to do something new even when you don't fully understand what that may look like?

ACTIVITY

Write a prayer to God and express gratitude for his continued blessings and favor in your life. Ask forgiveness for days you complained instead of praying and trusting God to make way for you.

Share your testimony of how God has showered you with favor and use it as an encouragement to restore someone's faith in God. For example, Daniel 4:2 says, "I thought it good to declare the signs and wonders that the Most High God has worked for me."

FIVE AFFIRMATIONS

1. God is good, and His love for me endures forever.

2. Despite trials and challenges, God's goodness sustains me and gives me hope.

3. I trust in God's goodness to guide me toward His perfect will for my life.

4. Each new day reminds me of God's goodness and faithfulness toward me.

5. As a daughter of God, I walk in the confidence that comes from knowing His goodness and mercy follow me throughout my life.

DEBORAH BLAKEY

OUTCOME JOURNAL

Chapter Six

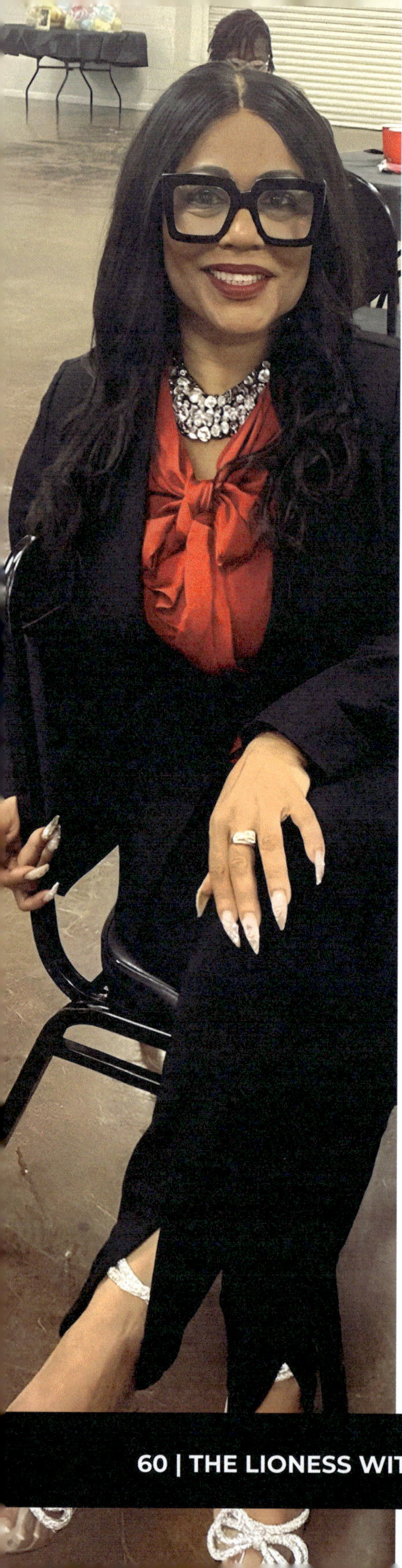

CHAPTER SIX:

ALL IN AND ALL OUT

As Christian women, we are called to live our lives in a way that honors God and reflects the love of Christ to those around us. It can be challenging to navigate the ups and downs of life while staying true to our faith, but with the Holy Spirit as our guide, we can walk in the fullness of God's plan for our lives.

Living for Christ means surrendering our desires and ambitions to God and allowing Him to lead us.

Living for Christ as a woman requires courage, strength, and perseverance, but with God on our side, we can overcome any obstacle that comes our way.

REFLECT ON THIS: REPRESENTING GOD ALL THE WAY

Reflect on a situation where the Lord reminded you that you were His. How did this impact your thoughts and actions at that moment?

1. What does it mean to be a representative of God in all we do? How does this impact our lives, decisions, and interactions with others?

2. How can you remind yourself daily that you are a representative of God? What practical steps can you take to keep this truth at the forefront of your mind and allow it to shape your actions and decisions?

3. Read 2 Corinthians 5:20-21. How does this passage reinforce the idea that we are representatives of God? How does it encourage you in your journey of representing Him well?

4. In what ways can you encourage and support other believers in their journey of representing God in all they do? How can you pray for and lift them in this area?

ACTIVITY

List three ways you have represented God well in your life that would encourage others.

FIVE AFFIRMATIONS

1. I am a chosen and beloved daughter of God, entrusted with the responsibility of representing Him to the world.

2. As I go about my daily life, I intentionally reflect God's love, grace, and truth to those around me.

3. Through the power of the Holy Spirit, I am empowered to live a life that honors God and inspires others to seek Him.

4. I am called to be a light in the darkness, bringing hope and healing to those who are hurting and lost.

5. In everything I do, I strive to bring glory to God and point others to Him, knowing that in Him, I have all that I need to live a life that honors Him.

Made in the USA
Columbia, SC
27 October 2023

24992611R00038

101

COSAS QUE DEBERÍAS SABER SOBRE

PERSONAJES DE LA CIENCIA

Dirección editorial: Ana Delgado
Textos: Giorgio Bergamino, Gianni Palitta
Traducción de: Herminia Bevia
Ilustraciones: Andrea Orani, Stefano Scagni
Preimpresión: Miguel Ángel San Andrés

C/ Campezo, 13 - 28022 Madrid
Tel.: 91 3009100 - 91 3009118
Impreso y encuadernado en España
www.susaeta.com

D.L.: M-26692-MMXVII

101

COSAS QUE DEBERÍAS SABER SOBRE

PERSONAJES DE LA CIENCIA

susaeta

Sumario

EL **MUNDO ANTIGUO**

1 ¿Qué inventó Eratóstenes?

Eratóstenes de Cirene (276-194 a. C.), director de la famosa Biblioteca de Alejandría, construyó un instrumento llamado «mesolabio» capaz de extraer raíces cúbicas, cálculo que servía para proyectar las grandes catapultas de torsión.

¿LO SABÍAS?

Durante el asedio de Siracusa, las máquinas de Arquímedes alzaron las naves romanas y las destruyeron.

2 ¿Quién midió la Tierra?

Eratóstenes fue famoso sobre todo por calcular el tamaño de la Tierra, y lo hizo empleando la trigonometría.

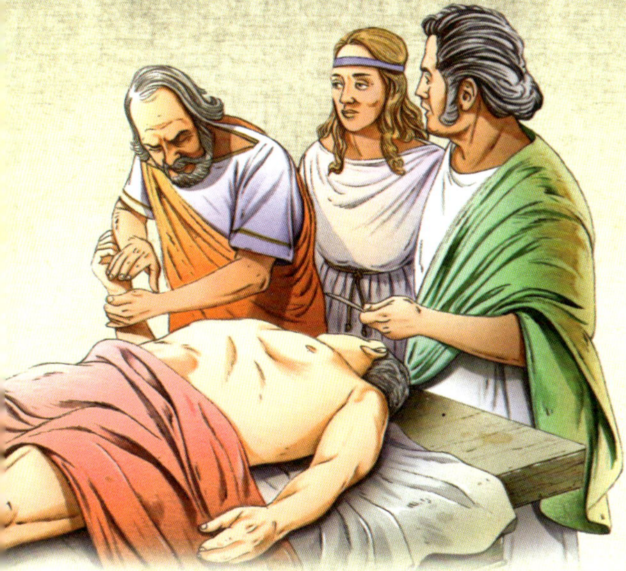

3 ¿Quién fue Herófilo?

Herófilo de Calcedonia (*ca.* 335-280 a. C.) fue un médico griego que descubrió los nervios. Estudiando la anatomía humana, los distinguió de los tendones y señaló el cerebro como centro de la inteligencia y del sistema nervioso.

4 ¿Por qué es Arquímedes uno de los científicos más famosos?

Arquímedes de Siracusa (287-212 a. C.) realizó importantes aportaciones en varios campos, desde la geometría y la matemática hasta la hidrostática, la óptica, la mecánica o la astronomía. Escribió muchas obras, y algunas se conservan.

5 ¿Quién es el padre de la geometría?

Se considera padre de la geometría al matemático griego Euclides (siglo III a. C.), que estudió las formas regulares (líneas, planos, círculos, triángulos, esferas, etc.).

6 ¿Quiénes fueron los mayores astrónomos del islam?

Varios científicos pueden ser considerados los más famosos e importantes de la ciencia islámica: Al-Farghani (*ca.* 800-870) estudió las dimensiones de la Tierra; Al-Juarismi (780-*ca.* 850) es tenido por el padre del álgebra moderna; y Al-Biruni (973-1048) estudió las proyecciones cartográficas.

7 ¿Quién dijo que la Tierra gira en torno al Sol?

Aristarco de Samos (310-230 a. C.) lo afirmó con una teoría que, según Plutarco, fue luego demostrada por Seleuco de Seleucia (190-*ca.* 150 a. C.).

8 ¿Cuántas estrellas catalogó Hiparco?

En su *Catálogo estelar*, por desgracia perdido, Hiparco de Nicea (200-120 a. C.) incluyó alrededor de 850 estrellas e indicó el grado de luminosidad de cada una y sus coordenadas en la esfera celeste.

9 ¿Quién habla del planetario de Arquímedes?

Cicerón (106-43 a. C.) describe este instrumento, que fue llevado a Roma por el cónsul Marcelo tras el saqueo de Siracusa (212 a. C.).

¿LO SABÍAS?

Los griegos hacían cálculos por medio de la geometría.

¿LO SABÍAS?

Arquímedes calculó cuántos granos de arena harían falta para llenar todo el Universo conocido.

10 ¿Quién pudo construir el mecanismo de Anticitera?

Según Cicerón, su amigo y maestro Posidonio de Rodas (135-50 a. C.) construyó un instrumento muy similar a esta asombrosa máquina capaz de predecir eclipses y posiciones astronómicas.

EL **CALENDARIO**

11 ¿Quién hizo el actual calendario?

Una comisión de expertos convocada en 1582 por el papa Gregorio XIII para reformar el calendario juliano, que llevaba en uso durante dieciséis siglos, se encargó de elaborar el calendario gregoriano, que ha sido adoptado en casi todo el mundo.

12 ¿Qué le caracteriza?

En el calendario gregoriano, son bisiestos aquellos años que son múltiplos de cuatro, excepto si terminan en dos ceros, en cuyo caso solo son bisiestos los múltiplos de cuatrocientos.

¿LO SABÍAS?

Antiguamente, muchos calendarios se basaban en los ciclos lunares.